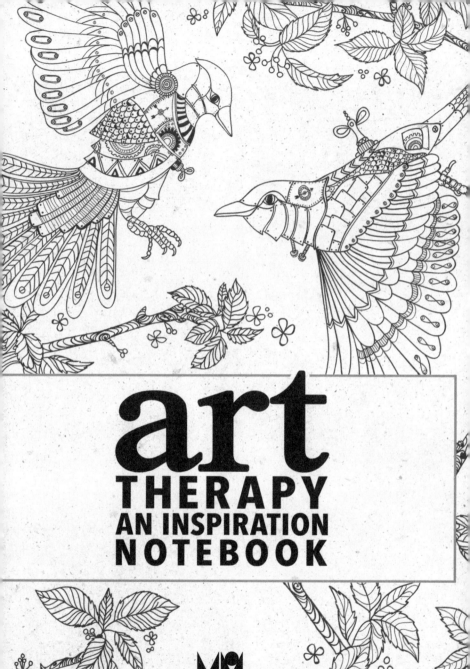

art
THERAPY
AN INSPIRATION
NOTEBOOK

Michael O'Mara Books Limited

Illustrated by
Sam Loman

Edited by Jonny Marx

Designed by Jack Clucas

Cover design by Angie Allison

With additional material adapted from www.shutterstock.com

First published in Great Britain in 2015 by Michael O'Mara Books Limited,
9 Lion Yard, Tremadoc Road, London SW4 7NQ

W www.mombooks.com
f Michael O'Mara Books
y @OMaraBooks

A CIP catalogue record for this book is available from the British Library.

ISBN: 978-1-78243-437-5

4 6 8 10 9 7 5 3

Printed by Leo Paper Products Ltd, Heshan Astros Printing Limited,
Xuantan Temple Industrial Zone, Gulao Town, Heshan City,
Guangdong Province, China.

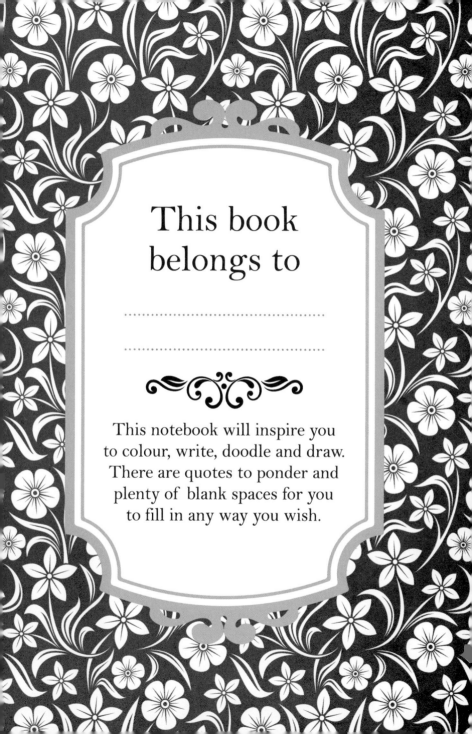

This book belongs to

....

....

This notebook will inspire you
to colour, write, doodle and draw.
There are quotes to ponder and
plenty of blank spaces for you
to fill in any way you wish.

'The greater danger for most of us lies not in setting our aim too high and falling short; but in setting our aim too low, and achieving our mark.'

Michelangelo

'Drawing is still basically the same as it has been since prehistoric times. It brings together man and the world. It lives through magic.'

Keith Haring

'Every portrait that is painted with feeling is a portrait of the artist, not of the sitter.'

Oscar Wilde

'You can't use up creativity. The more you use, the more you have.'

Maya Angelou

'Works of art, in my opinion, are the
only objects in the material universe
to possess internal order ...'

E. M. Forster

- ....
- ....
- ....
- ....
- ....
- ....
- ....
- ....
- ....
- ....
- ....
- ....
- ....
- ....
- ....
- ....

'If you want to conquer the anxiety of life,
live in the moment, live in the breath.'

Amit Ray

'Your scepticism will gradually diminish and your fear will turn to love … All art was modern once.'

Nicholas Serota

'In times of stress and adversity, it's always best to keep busy, to plow your anger and your energy into something positive.'

Lee Iacocca

'I strove with none; for none was worth my strife;
Nature I loved, and, next to Nature, Art.'

Walter Landor

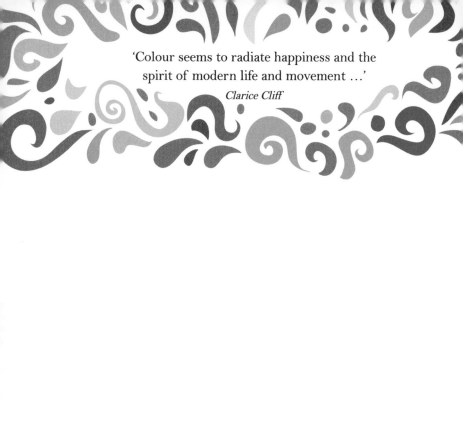

'Colour seems to radiate happiness and the spirit of modern life and movement …'

Clarice Cliff

'If you are distressed by anything external, the pain is not due to the thing itself, but to your estimate of it; and this you have the power to revoke at any moment.'

Marcus Aurelius

'A drawing is simply a line going for a walk.'

Paul Klee

'Mindfulness is simply being aware of what is happening right now without wishing it were different; enjoying the pleasant without holding on when it changes …'

James Baraz

'Painting is just another way of keeping a diary.'

Pablo Picasso

- ....

- ....

- ....

- ....

- ....

- ....

- ....

- ....

- ....

- ....

- ....

- ....

- ....

- ....

- ....

- ....

'Art is born of the observation and investigation of nature.'

Cicero

'Genius is one per cent inspiration,
ninety-nine per cent perspiration.'

Thomas Edison

'Stress should be a powerful
driving force, not an obstacle.'

Bill Phillips

- ....
- ....
- ....
- ....
- ....
- ....
- ....
- ....
- ....
- ....
- ....
- ....
- ....
- ....

- ....
- ....
- ....
- ....
- ....
- ....
- ....
- ....
- ....
- ....
- ....
- ....
- ....
- ....
- ....
- ....
- ....
- ....
- ....
- ....

'Art has no other end, for people
of feeling, than to conjure away
the burden and bitterness.'

Gustave Flaubert